COACH YOURSELF
BETTER, FAST

HOW TO BE HAPPY AT WORK

Based on *My Job Isn't Working!*
by Michael Brown

First published in Great Britain by Practical Inspiration Publishing, 2024

© Michael Brown and Practical Inspiration Publishing, 2024

The moral rights of the author have been asserted

ISBN   978-1-78860-667-7 (print)
           978-1-78860-669-1 (epub)
           978-1-78860-668-4 (Kindle)

All rights reserved. This book, or any portion thereof, may not be reproduced without the express written permission of the publisher.

Every effort has been made to trace copyright holders and to obtain their permission for the use of copyright material. The publisher apologizes for any errors or omissions and would be grateful if notified of any corrections that should be incorporated in future reprints or editions of this book.

Want to bulk-buy copies of this book for your team and colleagues? We can customize the content and co-brand *How to be Happy at Work* to suit your business's needs.

Please email info@practicalinspiration.com for more details.

Practical Inspiration Publishing

Contents

Series introduction iv

Introduction 1

Day 1: Reset your compass 3

Day 2: Build more trust: the CORE model 14

Day 3: Grow up 23

Day 4: Invest in relationships 34

Day 5: Negotiate for yourself 44

Day 6: Avoid avoidance 59

Day 7: Think! Working Smart model 71

Day 8: Listen more 79

Day 9: Meet intelligently 90

Day 10: Know yourself 102

Conclusion 110

Endnotes 117

Series introduction

Welcome to *6-Minute Smarts*!

This is a series of very short books with one simple purpose: to introduce you to ideas that can make life and work better, and to give you time and space to think about how those ideas might apply to *your* life and work.

Each book introduces you to ten powerful ideas, but ideas on their own are useless – that's why each idea is followed by self-coaching questions to help you work out the 'so what?' for you in just six minutes of exploratory writing. Because that's where the magic happens.

Whatever you're facing, there's a *6-Minute Smarts* book just for you. And once you've learned how to coach yourself through a new idea, you'll be smarter for life.

Find out more…

Introduction

I wonder what brought you to open this book? What might not be going as well for you as you'd like at work? Is something broken, or is it more a case of just wanting to get more happiness out of your job?

Whatever the reason, the good news is that you've come to the right place. In the coming pages you're going to find some tools and techniques you can use immediately that have been thoroughly road-tested and could well transform the way you feel about your job.

We're all being asked to do more with less again and again. There isn't enough time to think. Which means we never get round to doing those crucial things such as reviewing what went well on a project and what didn't. Meaning we don't learn: the same mistakes keep cropping up over and over, because we're too busy to find out why.

How to be Happy at Work

What about the relationships with the people you work with? You might see your boss regularly, but how often do you talk about what really matters?

My research tells me that people like you spend on average just two days per week doing what they think they're supposed to be doing. OMG! This means they're spending several days per week wasting time: probably in meetings they shouldn't be in, or on some process that doesn't work, or fighting through the email thicket.

There are so many ways you can rebuild your job happiness. Everything in this book is well within your capability. The only thing you're going to need to apply is some commitment to changing *your* behaviour. And that's going to take guts, a bit of courage and a willingness for it to feel a bit uncomfortable to start with. A bit like your first driving lessons: it feels weird, but eventually you won't have to remember to do it because it will be the way you do it. Simple.

Get yourself a 'feedback buddy', who can call you on it when you chicken out or slip back into bad habits. The more you share, the lighter the burden and the more likely you are to build some new habits.

You're ready to start. Over the next ten chapters (ten days, if you fancy treating this as a mini-course) you're going to discover ten key principles of how to be happy at work, and experiment with using them for yourself.

Let's go!

Day 1

Reset your compass

Introduction

Mid-career misery in the workplace needs to be tackled! Too many people who have worked more than a couple of years have lost sight of what's important, so it's important to reset your compass accordingly.

If you choose to try to improve your working environment, you have a chance of success. If you choose to believe that everything around you can't be changed and that you're powerless, it's a sure thing you'll prove yourself right.

Finding the point

There's nothing more dispiriting than grinding away at work when you can't see the point. Unless you can find a meaningful point to what you do and how it makes a difference, chances are you're not going to contribute your best. At the most extreme, people devoid of purpose deteriorate both mentally and physically. Today's workers are looking for meaningful and rewarding work, and are becoming increasingly demanding about the freedom they have to achieve the job's purpose.

People who are motivated perform better. Extrinsic motivators include bonuses, awards ceremonies, workplace relaxation devices and so on. Intrinsic motivation comes from within and is equally important; people who can't see the point of their work will never be intrinsically motivated.

Meaningfulness for yourself and others

I often ask people on my leadership courses a simple question: 'What's your purpose?'

They usually answer with 'to hit my target', 'to ensure continuity of supply', 'to launch new products successfully'. In other words, they tell me what they do. But not *what the point of it is*.

Typical corporate communication starts with describing what the organization does:

- 'We make the best batteries in the world.'

Reset your compass

- 'We have the lowest-priced rooms in town.'

But why would people care?

Simon Sinek says that compelling and inspirational communication starts with *why*, followed by *how* and then *what*. He calls his model The Golden Circle. [1]

THE GOLDEN CIRCLE

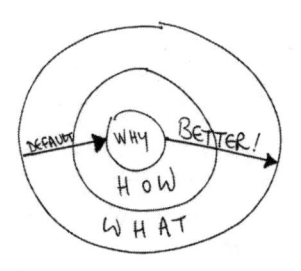

DEFAULT → WHY BETTER!
HOW
WHAT

He uses Apple as an example, as they happen to be good at this, and most people get what they try to do. This is how they communicate:

> 'Everything we do, we believe in challenging the status quo. We believe in thinking differently.'
>
> (WHY)

'The way we challenge the status quo is by making our products beautifully designed, simple to use and user-friendly.'

(HOW)

'We happen to make great computers.'

(WHAT)

Too many organizations do this the other way round. They tell the world how great they are (WHAT they do) and maybe HOW they achieve it, but they rarely go on to define WHY they do it. This is uninspiring and doesn't cause others to follow.

Many people I've met over the years haven't got a WHY. How do I know this? Well, in most of the workshops I run I ask them to self-assess on three questions, where 10 is high in all of them:

1. How productive are you? Average answer = 7 nudging 6.
2. How stressed are you? Average answer = 7.
3. How much of your potential is unlocked in your current role? Average answer = 6 nudging 7.

This is a story of averageness – it's not high performance and it's certainly not job fulfilment or high motivation. (I'd argue it's a pretty high average level of stress, too.)

The WHY

So – what's your WHY? What gets you out of bed in the morning?

I often work with groups, asking them to define a WHY for themselves and their teams. Possibly the best example I ever heard was a finance director of a small technology company, whose WHY was 'making finance easy'. Every decision he and his team have to make is now assessed against how much easier it will make life for their colleagues in the business. This reference point gives everyone something to aim at.

The majority of people I've met over the years have never considered this question and as a result are missing out on a big boost to their career mojos.

Understanding where you fit

Not knowing how your contribution fits within the organization could lead to:

- **Not knowing what's important:** If you don't know what's important, how can you prioritize?
- **Not being able to collaborate:** If you don't know what others around you are trying to achieve, it's hard to collaborate.
- **Not being seen as relevant:** I'd argue that if you don't find out where you fit, you have only yourself to blame if you get overlooked for that promotion.

Let's think practically:

1. **Check your job description:** If you don't have one, do something about it. Write it and get it approved and make sure HR are involved. If you do have one, check that it's still up to date and reflects what you do. Review it annually.
2. **Ask to see your boss's job description:** If you know what your boss is measured on, you already have a sense of what's important to them.
3. **Find out your organization's strategy:** You should be able to articulate the top three things the organization is seeking to achieve this year.

4. **Map out your stakeholder landscape:** Make a list of the top ten people you need to engage with or who are impacted by what you do.

Be clear about what's important to you

What attracted you to your job in the first place? Has this been lost somehow? Or it may have changed. Starting a family, for example, often triggers a shift in priorities. Having more personal time so you can see your children grow up is the most obvious example.

- **Values:** What are my core values that I cherish most deeply?
- **Alignment:** How do my values align with the organization's espoused values?
- **Purpose:** Do I have a clear purpose?
- **Pride:** How proud am I of what I do?
- **Persistence:** How well do I follow through on what I say I'm going to do?

I believe Values is the most important of these. When your values are different to someone else's, you're in a conflict situation, which can be difficult or perhaps impossible to resolve.

Clarify your personal goals

Imagine yourself three years from now. (If that's too far, come back to one year.) Ask yourself these questions:

- What do I want?
- How will I know when I've achieved it?
- What will I be doing then that I'm not doing now?
- Where and with whom will I be doing it?
- How will it enhance my life?
- How will I be feeling?
- What are the five areas I need to work on in order to achieve this?
- What are the first steps I need to take on the five areas?
- When will I take them?

Describe to someone you trust the actions you plan to take. Your commitment will increase and that person can support you and hold you accountable. Keep the plan visible and review it regularly.

How long are you prepared to wait for something to change?

So what? Over to you...

1. What has resonated most with you in this chapter?

2. Who can you talk to at work about your thoughts? In particular, how can you start to share your thinking with your boss?

Reset your compass

3. How will you keep the goals you've identified at the front of your mind, and check in on your progress?

Day 2

Build more trust: the CORE model

Trust at work

When you have high levels of trust, you can collaborate, you can deal with change, you can build a truly high-performance team. Trust takes years to build and seconds to destroy.

Research tells us that there's a strong link between trust levels and employee engagement. Trust also impacts on productivity: researchers at the University of Sheffield found that high trust levels lead to productivity levels 5% above the average.[2] Sadly, the research also tells us that trust levels are on the slide.

Build more trust: the CORE model

Why are trust levels so weak?

We're becoming less trusting. Doing what you say you're going to do is a key component in building trust. We've all seen what faking it looks like; politicians are particularly adept at it – it destroys our respect for them.

Social media's intrusion into our lives causes us to spend time communicating through our devices when we should be talking to each other and building trust. We check our devices too often, we let them intrude on important conversations, we broadcast messages but fail to communicate. This is a widely acknowledged dysfunction in society, leading to a breakdown in relationships, which itself breaks down levels of trust.

Two other important factors that mitigate against high levels of trust include:

- **Shortage of time:** The 'more with less' mantra shows there simply is no slack in the system. If you can't anticipate the next crisis before it hits you, you're less likely to invest time in exploring options with a colleague when a conflict arises.

- **Remote working:** This may be from home or from a different country (and time zone potentially). If you rarely (or sometimes never) get to meet people in person, it's far harder to get to know them. When your communication is at best via a video call or at worst via email or some internal chat application, it's easy for it to be misinterpreted. If I misinterpret your communication, you may question my competence, it may produce conflict or chaos, and we're not going to trust each other as we did before.

In conclusion, we see trust levels breaking down in society as a whole. We compound the problem with our behaviours, and because we feel less secure in our jobs, we feel less inclined to open up with other people.

What's the impact?

If we don't trust someone, we feel threatened. Our brains switch into defensive mode and we seek to protect ourselves. In one way or another we'll display Fight, Flight or Freeze responses, which are hardly the ingredients for a collaborative and high-performing team.

Build more trust: the CORE model

We cover our backs with an auditable trail of email and documentation just in case anyone should point the finger at us. What a time-waster!

The CORE model of trust

In order for you to trust me, I need to build up four trust elements in your mind. Think of the CORE of an apple to remember this one:

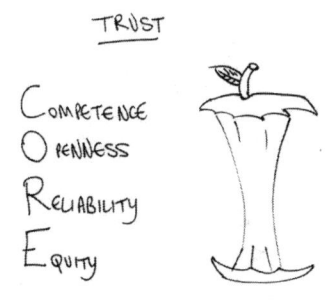

TRUST

Competence
Openness
Reliability
Equity

- **Competence:** I need to demonstrate competence quickly – you need to see me as the right person to talk to. I need to show you I know my stuff, have done my preparation and maybe have done this before.
- **Openness:** If you're to trust me, I need to be open with you. Closed behaviour (such as whispering) will cause you not to trust me.

If I don't say much, or avoid your questions, you might not trust me. If I refuse to share information, or keep things from you, it can damage trust.
- **Reliability:** Doing what you say you're going to do. Walking the talk. Being consistent and predictable. These are all things that will build trust. You only have to let someone down once and you can severely damage a relationship. Do it twice and you can do it for life.
- **Equity:** This means fairness. Our relationship has to be fair if you're going to trust me. It has to be a two-way street. I give you something, you give me something back.

Using the CORE model

The CORE model really works:

- It build relationships and trust.
- It makes negotiation less competitive and stressful.

If you don't have a trusting relationship with your boss, it's essential that you fix it by using CORE to support your relationship.

Build more trust: the CORE model

Try being open with an emotion; for instance, 'I'm a bit confused as I've not come across this before.' Often, the other person will reciprocate and you can then build on this by being open on something more important, and again they may reciprocate – the relationship becomes less guarded and you move towards a much more honest and meaningful dialogue.

You can plan your Reliability. Only commit to something you can guarantee you can deliver on. Doing this regularly means you show you're a trustworthy person.

Finally, be aware of the need for Equity. Make an effort to give back whenever you can. Be the first to make a move. The chances are the other party will give you something back when you do. 'Reciprocity', as this might be called, is well proven as a tool for influence. Kindness breeds kindness.

However, as we work towards high levels of trust, we don't want to be open about everything, so we need to think about what we can disclose that will move towards increased openness while at the same time not undermining our credibility. You might win Openness points for saying 'I have no idea how that happened', while losing points on the Competence scale.

It's risky, though, if you display Openness and the other party doesn't reciprocate. Win/win always requires a degree of courage. It's called leadership.

Developing trusting relationships with your colleagues and stakeholders is like putting top-quality oil in your mojo engine. If people trust you, things will run so much more smoothly. You can afford the occasional cock-up if people trust you, because we're all human. Mess up too often and it's a different story, of course. But for now, have a think about how trusting you are of others and where you need to focus some more effort.

So what? Over to you...

1. What erodes trust in your workplace?

Build more trust: the CORE model

2. Who do you need to build a trusting relationship with, and why?

3. How can you use the CORE principles to develop that level of trust?

Day 3

Grow up

Analysing your transactions

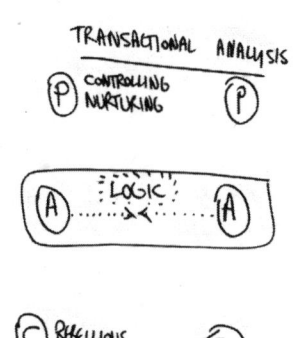

TRANSACTIONAL ANALYSIS

(P) CONTROLLING / NURTURING   (P)

(A) ....LOGIC.... (A)

(C) REBELLIOUS / INNOCENT   (C)

Let me introduce you to Transactional Analysis. At any one moment in time you and I have an ego state: a set of thoughts, feelings and behaviours that creates a personality style. At any one time we can be either a Parent (P), Adult (A) or Child (C).

Styles of Parent

- **Controlling:** 'Ring me when you get there, and make sure you're back before midnight.'
- **Nurturing:** 'Have a lovely time, and say hi to Joe's mum for me.'

Nurturing Parents allow the Child to play and learn and set fewer rules for them.

Adult state

This is how we regulate our Parent and Child states, and the state in which we remain objective. When two Adults are 'transacting', the exchange will have more logic and less emotion than in the other two states. For many, it's our 'ideal self'.

Grow up

Styles of Child

- **Rebellious Child (noisy or silent):** The ones with an agenda, and who are generally trouble to deal with. You tell the noisy ones you deal with to leave the table and go to their room; the silent have long faces and won't engage unless you make them. You know the sort.
- **Innocent Child:** Are fun to be with, and they like to learn through play and just being children. They have no agenda and are happy to be guided on what to do and what not to do.

A time and place for all ego states

All three ego states have a role to play in the workplace. You flip in and out of them from minute to minute, and much of the time this is fine.

1. We need a Parent in the room when we need someone to chair the disciplinary meeting for the employee who broke the security protocols, for example.
2. Adult-to-Adult transactions are great where we want to discuss things freely: where there's no right or wrong and we want to involve people

on an equal power footing. A great way to hold a coaching conversation. Great for team problem-solving.
3. Child ego state may unlock creativity, intuition, spontaneous drive and fun. Denying this can lead to loss of curiosity, or of the ability to dream.

Analysing transactions

Think of a recent transaction you had with someone and try to work out what the ego states were (both yours and the other party's). How was the other person's ego state influencing yours, and vice versa?

Was their ego state a response to yours, or was it the other way round? If I become your Parent, it's very hard for you not to become my Child.

Where did it all go wrong?

Like many things in life, when you get the timing wrong it can lead to problems. Workplace dysfunctionality can come about when we get crossed wires, which we don't want, or where the ego state is wrong for the situation.

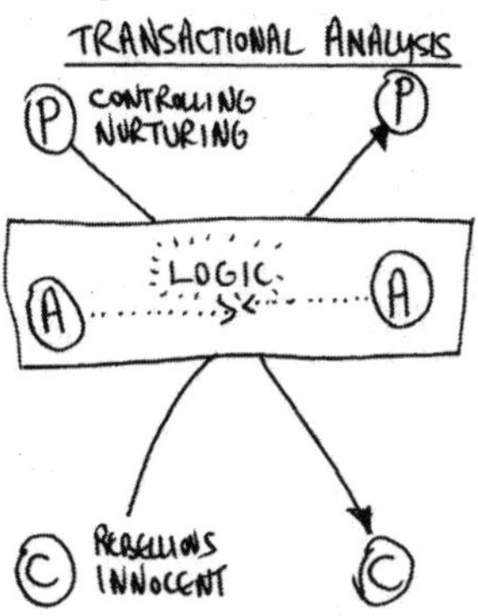

Grow up

TRANSACTIONAL ANALYSIS

[Diagram: Two boxes side by side, each containing P (Parent - Controlling/Nurturing) at top, A (Adult - Logic) in middle, and C (Child - Rebellious/Innocent) at bottom. Arrows cross from the left Parent to the right Parent, and from the left Child to the right Child, with Adult-to-Adult logic connection in the middle.]

How many Children in your team?

Some people are so used to being handled by a Parent that they give up trying to do Adult, as they find it too dispiriting. It's far easier just to sit back, relax and wait to be told what to do. But this causes the Parent to have to do even more Parenting, and leads to micromanagement by the Parent and disengagement by the Child.

If these people could regain their Adult ego state when they need it, they might be capable of so much more and undoubtedly they'd find more satisfaction and happiness while at work.

What brings out the Child in you?

Does your Child come out to play at work when perhaps it shouldn't? If so, why?

- Is there someone who, by virtue of their seniority, expertise, experience or class, just somehow makes you feel inferior? Maybe not deliberately perhaps, but somehow they just do?
- Do you need to be more in control? Do you need more time to prepare? Do you need more information?
- Do you disagree with something but don't feel you can voice it?
- Do you feel disempowered because of where you work (from home, in another time zone, not on the same continent as HQ)?
- Do you feel vulnerable because you don't understand the jargon or there's a language barrier?
- Do you carry the label of being new to the role for too long – almost as a security blanket?

It's a choice

Your ego state is a choice you make. You can choose to respond to others in a Child way: no one can force you.

It's a decision you make in the millisecond you have before you respond to that trigger, be it an annoying email or a rude comment made in a meeting.

Slow down and pause before responding – there's always more than one response available to you.

How to get out of the playground

And so to the crux of it. If you recognize where your Child ego state is getting in the way of a fruitful relationship, and you've identified some triggers, we now just need to know how to adapt our behaviour so we can get out of the playground.

While you can't change the other person (and neither should you try to), you can change their response to you. To do that you have to change your behaviour – and you are totally in control of that decision.

That means you need to make the first move. Be proactive, and be ready to take the risk of making the first move of applying an Adult mindset. If it helps, become the person you most admire for their Adult attitudes.

You might want to think through how your amended transaction is going to sound. Visualize it. Role play it with a friend even.

- 'Boss, I was hoping we could meet up so we could discuss an idea I have,' becomes: 'John, I have a proposal I think you'd want to see. Can we meet at two for ten minutes to go through it?'

If your Child is triggered, for instance when making a presentation and realizing there are experts in the room, the best way to defuse them is to acknowledge them as experts. Then they don't have to prove it by asking you nasty questions. Try inserting this type of language into the opening of your next presentation:

- 'I know there's a lot of experience and expertise in the room today, and I really want to make sure we use that, so please feel free to add in where relevant as I go through the presentation.'

Now that they feel acknowledged, they're on your side. You've made yourself bulletproof.

Similarly, a great way to get Parents who are doing Parent as a power statement to become Adult is to acknowledge them. This can be done with language, quite subtly:

- 'Clearly this is your decision, but here are the two options I'd recommend.'

Grow up

Many of your unsatisfactory transactions can probably be characterized as some form of 'crossed wire' (a Parent–Child transaction where you are Child and wish you could get to Adult, but can't).

You *can* fix this! It just takes a bit of courage and some thinking through.

So what? Over to you...

1. Think about the Parent transactions you have that put you in Child mode at work. How can you make the first move to shift these towards Adult transactions?

2. If you're being a Parent towards someone else, how might you create a more Adult-to-Adult relationship with that person?

3. What does your inner Child look, sound and feel like? How might you calm it when it wakes up at work?

Day 4
Invest in relationships

Introduction

When you have too much to do and not enough time to do it, one of the first things to suffer is the time you invest in building relationships, which is essential for a well-functioning career mojo.

Assess yourself

You have to earn relationships. If your boss has a habit of cancelling your one-to-one meetings at the last minute, which leaves you feeling annoyed and undervalued, give them some feedback about this, otherwise you're perpetuating a dysfunctional relationship.

Invest in relationships

The really important relationships have to be based on mutual understanding of what's important, some agreed goals, agreed ways of working and so on. If you don't know what's important, you live a life of what I call 'spray and pray': rushing around doing lots of activity in the hope that some of it will be seen as useful and relevant. A recipe for burnout and mojo loss.

Making time for it

Plan your time and ring-fence it (using the usual techniques: book a meeting with yourself, schedule meetings with people in which the agenda is to look at how you can work more effectively together).

What does good look like?

Good relationships are built by deploying emotional intelligence. In these relationships, people are able to open up with each other and let their humanity out. They genuinely care about the other person and are honest, vulnerable and sincere towards them. They can see the other person's perspective, and even if they don't agree with it, they can understand it and empathize with it. Conflict levels are low because

Getting closer to your boss

You have the right to a regular, constructive one-to-one meeting with your boss, ideally once per month. Plan these well in advance. (You could even schedule them for the whole year – these are important meetings, so why not get them in the schedule before others do?) Allow one hour.

Plan the agenda and send it in advance. This shows you value the meeting and are being proactive. If your boss is an introvert, they'll appreciate having time to consider it in advance of the meeting, and you'll have shown respect. If you show someone respect, you usually get respect back.

Don't fill all the time with reviewing your progress against the previous to-do list. You can do that with a spreadsheet and send it before or after the meeting. Instead use it to cover much more important questions, such as:

- What are your current priorities? What's on your mind?

Invest in relationships

- What are your objectives and how can I best support them? How does what I do fit into the bigger picture?
- What would you like me to do more of and less of?
- How else could I increase my contribution to our success?
- What feedback do you have for me?
- How can you support my personal growth?
- What contingencies should we be planning for?
- What do you know that I should be aware of?

You should walk away from these discussions with a clear understanding of what's important and how you can add value to your contribution. This allows you to prioritize and push back on non-important requests.

Get yourself some decent objectives

The idea behind setting annual objectives is to produce clarity over what's required and to give the individual something motivational to work towards.

- Recognize the difference between a goal, a target and an objective. Well-formed objectives are initiatives you'll undertake that will contribute to the achievement of the objectives your boss is working towards. Goals set out what you're seeking to accomplish. Targets are measures of success.
- Be proactive. Propose your objectives at a timely discussion with your boss, before the corporate stuff lands. By all means keep their targets to hand as well, of course, but the motivational stuff will be the key initiatives you agree between you as being most relevant and meaningful for the coming year.
- Don't set more than five objectives. Cognitive overload kicks in after five. Go for the five things you feel most motivated about and that you agree will make the most positive impact on your boss's achievements.
- Make sure you align with your boss! Start by asking to see a copy of their objectives and use that to inform where you should focus your energy.
- Keep the objectives SMART: Specific, Measurable, Agreed, Relevant and Timebound. The more concrete and granular the objective, the more likely it is to work.

Invest in relationships

- Treat them as organic. Rarely, if ever, will an objective agreed in December still be relevant 12 months later. Chances are you'll have achieved it or things will have changed and it's no longer relevant.
- Keep them visible. Physically put these five initiatives where you see them regularly. I have mine printed out and stuck to the pen holder on my desk.

Where to start?

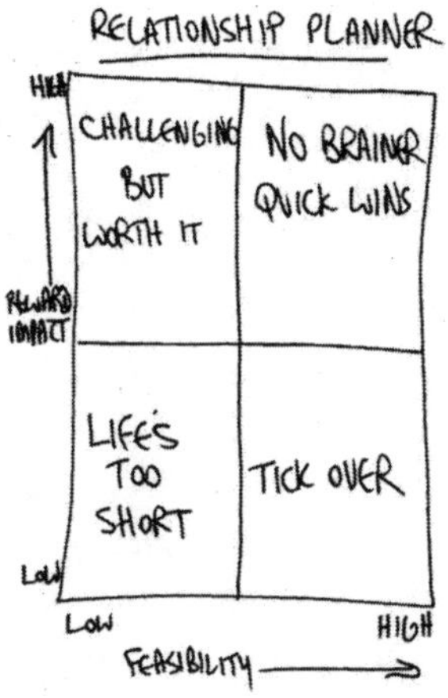

RELATIONSHIP PLANNER

	Low Feasibility	High Feasibility
High Reward/Impact	CHALLENGING BUT WORTH IT	NO BRAINER QUICK WINS
Low Reward/Impact	LIFE'S TOO SHORT	TICK OVER

You need to know which relationships to prioritize. Look at the benefit versus the effort required to build the relationship. Try using this relationship to help you identify who is in the No-Brainer Quick Wins box – these are people where making this investment is important because of the impact they have in your working life, and where it's feasible for you to achieve this improvement. Identify three people in the top-right box.

A plea for more humanity

Allow more time to check in with people at the beginning of a meeting – to celebrate a success or acknowledge and empathize with someone else's difficulties.

Treat your break at lunchtime as an opportunity to catch up with a colleague you haven't seen for a while. Or pick up the phone and talk to someone who helped you out a while back and has since gone quiet.

It's very easy to find a reason not to do these things, so it's a matter of making the effort to stay connected. Just because no one measures this and it goes on behind the scenes is no reason not to do it.

Invest in relationships

✏️ So what? Over to you…

1. How is your relationship with your boss working, and how might you make it work better?

2. How are your objectives working, and how might you make them work better?

Invest in relationships

3. How can you go about improving the relationships with the three people in your 'no-brainer-quick-wins' box?

Day 5

Negotiate for yourself

Introduction

Negotiation is, without doubt, a critical life skill. The good news is that successful negotiation is not so much about technique as it is about mindset.

A few guiding principles

- Not everything is negotiable, but you can negotiate a lot more than you might think.
- Don't waste time trying to negotiate the non-negotiable. Put your energy into battles you can win.
- Negotiation is something you have to practise. Think of it as a muscle that you need to build by doing it regularly.

Negotiate for yourself

- If you negotiate well, it improves relationships. Some people shy away from it because they fear it will make them unpopular. The opposite is the case.
- If you don't test other people's positions, you may leave opportunities on the table – very often the other person doesn't expect you to agree immediately.
- It's not possible to function effectively at work without using negotiation.
- There's risk involved as it takes courage to offer alternative options rather than saying 'yes' to something straight away.

Why don't we negotiate more?

Tell yourself that negotiating is being helpful and is a form of leadership required of all of us. If you negotiate well and are looking for win/win outcomes, the other party will benefit as well.

What if we don't negotiate?

If you don't negotiate, your situation won't change. You attend meetings you know are a waste of time because you didn't negotiate. You take on work you know you shouldn't because you don't negotiate. You say yes to things that impinge upon your personal time because you don't negotiate.

It's all in the mind!

Good negotiation is about mindset and I'm going to share a real-life experience with you. How would you have handled it?

> It was a cold night in February and I was staying in a fancy hotel in Edinburgh. At 3am the fire alarms went off, so I threw on a few clothes and went outside to stand on the frosty pavement for 30 minutes while the fire brigade established it was a false alarm. I went back to bed and didn't get back to sleep.
>
> At 7am I got up and discovered there was no hot water, so it was a cold shower and a cold shave to start the day. I was not a happy bunny.
>
> What would you (honestly now!) have said when you went to check out that morning? I use this exercise when I run negotiation courses, and I can tell you that the range of responses goes from:

Negotiate for yourself

- Nothing, I'd just never use that hotel again.
- I'd ask for a £50 refund.
- Refuse to pay anything and demand a voucher for a future stay to compensate for my inconvenience.

The range of what I call 'mental limits' on this particular scenario is £0 through to £300. Those mental limits – the voice that tells you what something is worth, or indeed whether something is negotiable – are self-imposed. You acquire your mental limits from seeing how others around you negotiate, or your culture, or the type of work you do. They inform the way you go about negotiating.

Recognize that your personal mental limits might be inhibiting you – the best thing is to find out what the other person's mental limits are first. They're probably different from yours.

This is what I did in the hotel that day.

'Good morning, room 35 checking out please. You're probably aware there was no hot water this morning. I was wondering what you can do to put that right for me?'

'I'm so sorry, Mr Brown, let me have a word with my colleague.' (Scurries off, returns with duty manager – a good sign.)

'Mr Brown, we do apologize, this always seems to happen when we have a fire alarm go off. I expect you'd like me to write off last night's bill?'

As my mental limits had been telling me my discomfort was worth a £50 voucher, I graciously accepted the £150 offered and departed. I should probably have said it was a good start, now what about something for the inconvenience?!

The technique is therefore to ask questions to find out the other person's mental limit before you tell them yours. Once you've decided what your position is going to be on something, add (or deduct) 20% further. You'll often get it!

Negotiating collaboratively

When we're trying to negotiate collaboratively and want the other party to feel good about the outcome, we need to get past defensive reactions so that we can explore things together. So we need to use signals and language that help the other party not to feel threatened.

Negotiate for yourself

Avoid triggering a defensive response if you possibly can. My suggestion is that you make a real effort to acknowledge the other person. Create an atmosphere of collaboration based on mutual respect by making it obvious that you're acknowledging them as well. You can signal this with some of the language you use, for example:

> 'I completely understand why you might feel that way.'

Once you acknowledge the other person, it takes the heat out of the situation. Use open questions to get the other party talking, then offer a well-signalled summary to demonstrate that you've been listening and to remove any misunderstandings:

> 'Let me see if I've understood you correctly. You're asking me to come in again this weekend to help us catch up on the project. You don't think there's anyone else you could ask as this needs my specific input, and you're aware this is the third time you've asked me to do this. Have I missed anything, or is this a good summary of the situation?

(The added benefit of this type of summary is that if it's a negotiation about something unreasonable, the other party gets to hear the unreasonable request for themselves and it might cause them to rethink it as you're playing it back to them. It's also buying you some time to calm down and start thinking straight again.)

Handling objections

The acknowledgement technique works very well when you're thrown an objection. This might be in a negotiation or when you're pitching an idea in a meeting. Objections are a good thing, by the way, as they show the other party is listening and is still engaged.

Three-step approach to handling an objection

PAUSE – ACKNOWLEDGE – PROBE

- **Pause:** Gives you a moment to think and stop yourself going into defensive mode. It's also hard to think and talk at the same time.
- **Acknowledge:** Defuses the objection and builds respect; people who show respect usually get it back. 'Thanks for raising that.'

'I can see why that might be a concern.' 'I hear you.'
- **Probe:** Involves asking open questions to try to find out what lies at the heart of the objection. 'How much of a concern is that?' 'Why is that such a concern?' 'If we can deal with that concern are you happy to sign?' Often these questions will help you to find a way through.

Creative negotiating

When you're trying to negotiate on things that affect your mojo (workload, pay and reward, etc.), you'll probably be negotiating with someone with whom you have an ongoing relationship. Therefore win/win is probably the best mode to be in. Win/lose is unlikely to be a good mode because if you get what you want and they don't, you may damage the relationship and they may get you back later. People have long memories.

Finding a win/win requires two ingredients – courage and creativity:

- Courage because we need to engage in what's not always an easy conversation, and many people simply don't like negotiating.

- Creativity because win/win isn't always obvious and we may have to think outside the box a bit.

Here's a tool to help with creativity. I call it the Deal Juggler. There are four devices to help you find creative answers to your negotiation. Let's use negotiating a salary increase as an example to explain the tool.

Imagine you haven't had a salary increase for three years and are trying to negotiate a 5% increase starting next month. You've reached an impasse – the boss has said there's nothing she can do as her salary increase budget has already been used up for the year. Whip out your Deal Juggler and try one of these:

- **Make it smaller:** Negotiate a three-month interim increase instead of a 12-month one by way of a project bonus, to tide you over until the next salary year when the budget becomes available again.
- **Make it bigger:** Defer the increase until the next salary year but have it backdated to now and locked in for two successive years.
- **Change the mix:** Add in some extra components. Talk about a mix of extra money,

training, holiday, car allowance. These come out of different pots but they're all money.
- **Turn it upside down:** Instead of talking about salary, talk about job role. Workload. Holiday. Pension. Bonus. Car. School fees. For example, maybe you can defer having a new company car next year and instead get more money.

A simple but effective assertiveness tool

Mojo loss can occur when you're not assertive enough to say what you really want to. I've learned various techniques to help me deal with my natural lack of assertiveness, one of which is to use a very short and simple word: *If*.

> Inserting *if* into your response when someone asks you to do something turns it instantly into a negotiation. It can lead to much better outcomes.

> 'Can you get the report finished by Friday, Mike?'

> 'Sure, *if* you can do the executive summary and are happy to do the slides for Monday.'

Giving yourself more power

Never negotiate without a BANANA in your pocket. It's an acronym (sort of) for Best AlterNative to A Negotiated Agreement.

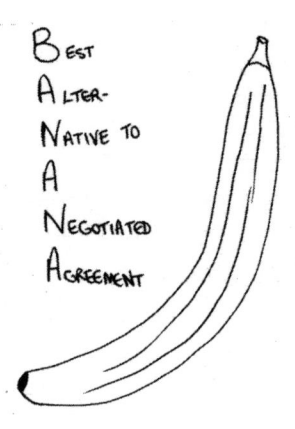

Best
Alter-
Native to
A
Negotiated
Agreement

A BANANA is something you plan in advance – doing so will give you the option to walk away when you need to. It's the best alternative to doing a deal that day, with that person, on those terms.

Let's say you're buying a car. BANANAs you could plan in advance might include:

- Don't buy one at all. Do without until next year.

Negotiate for yourself

- Buy one from somewhere else.
- Buy a different model.
- Buy a motorbike instead.

If you don't have a BANANA in your pocket, you risk doing a deal you shouldn't do (because you have no alternative).

So when you're negotiating and you need to get the best deal, spend a bit of time planning your opening position (a good rule of thumb is to aim 10% higher than you expect to achieve) and know what your walk-away point should be – then work out your walk-away options.

Negotiation hints and tips

Try out the 'Nothing for Nothing' mindset. Try not to give away anything for nothing. People don't value free stuff, so make it look expensive.

Slow down your response. Allow a pause in the negotiation, so it looks as if you're weighing things up. Make notes, do come calculations. People will respect a 'considered response' more than a quick one. It's also helpful because it gives you time to think and devise alternative options.

Recognize the power of Anchoring. This is about defining the negotiation playing field by going first with an aggressive opening offer. Research tells us that the deliberately low (or high, depending on whether you're buying or selling) offer will lead directly to better results for the person who opens the bidding.

What to do if someone low- (or high-) balls you? Respond quickly with an equally aggressive counter-bid. It balances the power in the equation. Or alternatively whip out your BANANA, assuming you have one (e.g. by walking away).

So what? Over to you...

1. How comfortable are you with the idea of negotiating? Why is that?

Negotiate for yourself

2. Think about a current or upcoming situation where you have to negotiate: how might you approach this more creatively?

3. What are your BANANAs for that negotiation?

Day 6
Avoid avoidance

Introduction

Conflict is a good thing. Without it there would be no learning, no change, no progress. People often see conflict as something to be avoided because they worry about being seen as a troublemaker but this leads to the same mistakes being repeated over and over again, weak or non-existent levels of feedback, and huge amounts of time wasted in meetings.

The avoidance default at work

One of the reasons you may not feel comfortable with conflict at work is the way others around you behave. Ralph Kilmann and Ken Thomas (the Thomas-

Kilmann Conflict Mode Instrument (TKI), 1971), devised five preferences: Competing, Collaborating, Compromising, Accommodating and Avoiding.[3] Kilmann established that, in the workplace, Avoiding is the preferred mode for resolving conflict.

A diagnostic exercise

Let's explore a model that will help you understand your response to conflict more fully by carrying out a short – honestly answered – exercise:

- Write down the least lawful thing you've ever done. (Note: speeding fines and parking tickets don't count.)
- Done it? Great. We'll come back to what you wrote in a moment.

A useful conflict model

The TKI model is based on the premise that we all have a personal preference for how we respond in a conflict situation. We can use our non-preferred response, but under pressure and in the heat of the moment, our preferred response is the most likely to present itself.

Avoid avoidance

CONFLICT PREFERENCES

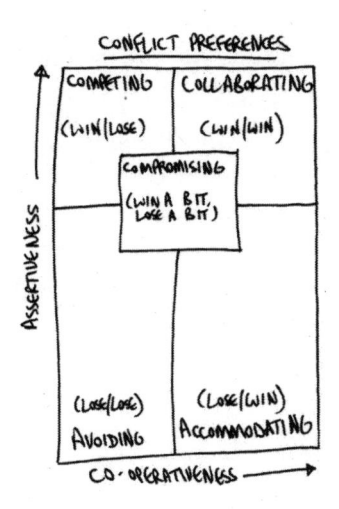

A hand-drawn 2x2 matrix with Assertiveness on the vertical axis and Co-operativeness on the horizontal axis:
- Top-left: COMPETING (WIN/LOSE)
- Top-right: COLLABORATING (WIN/WIN)
- Centre: COMPROMISING (WIN A BIT, LOSE A BIT)
- Bottom-left: AVOIDING (LOSE/LOSE)
- Bottom-right: ACCOMMODATING (LOSE/WIN)

The model shows five conflict modes, each of which varies based on the extent to which, when under pressure, you're concerned with what other people need (Co-operativeness) or how much you're concerned with your own needs (Assertiveness).

You learn over time how to deal with conflict – from others around you, where you work, the nature of your work and so on. Maybe your boss encourages a certain style, or other styles are frowned on in your organization. Chances are these might influence your personal 'defaults' when there's conflict around.

How to be Happy at Work

Earlier, I asked you to write down the least lawful thing you've ever done. Let's use your answer to try to work out what your preference is.

- **Accommodator:** Did you do as instructed but felt uncomfortable about it? Maybe you wrote down a truthful answer but were then glad you used a pencil so you could rub it out (because it's incriminating evidence!). Did you comply with my request because I issued it and I'm in charge here?
- **Avoider:** Maybe you didn't do it at all? Maybe you wrote down something that wasn't true, or something that was unlawful but not the most unlawful thing you've ever done?
- **Competer:** Perhaps you proudly wrote down something that was true but knowing that under no circumstances would you share what you'd written. You'd have met the challenge I set but will have a plan for how to get the better of me if necessary.
- **Compromiser:** Perhaps you like to find workable solutions when there's conflict around but not spend all night over it. So you might have written something a bit illegal – something that might go along with the exercise in order to get the learning from it,

Avoid avoidance

but you shied away from revealing the truly illegal thing you did; that is, working with me, but not revealing your complete hand.

- **Collaborator:** Maybe you went with the exercise despite feeling uncomfortable because you were prepared to take a risk in order to get the maximum return from your investment in this book. So you might have written down the truth but would draw the line if I said the next stage of the exercise is to email me what you wrote. If we'd been face to face, you may have asked questions such as 'what's in it for me?' and if you were satisfied that there was a benefit from taking the risk, you'd have been happy to do so.

People tend to become more comfortable with Competing and Collaborating over time. Business leaders need to be okay with unpopular decisions at times (Competing) and need to be able to sit down and work out win/win solutions when the stakes are high and we need a long-term solution (Collaborating).

Collaborating is found in equal measure across both genders. However, males are significantly more competitive at all ages than females.

Consciously choosing which mode to be in for a given situation can be a great time-saver.

A time and place for all styles

High Assertiveness

COMPETING
- No relationship needed
- Important to win
- Short of time

COLLABORATING
- Long term relationship
- Time available
- Worth the effort

COMPROMISE
- Collaboration not possible
- Lack of time

AVOIDING
- Not worth it
- Need more time
- Wrong time

ACCOMMODATING
- To help win next time
- Build relationship
- Not important

Low Assertiveness

Low ← Co-operativeness → High

It can be okay to compete when you don't ever need to talk to the person again, or don't need to care about them – like annoying salespeople who ring me at home on a Friday evening! Also I might go Competitive if the house is on fire, or if someone is threatening my family (high stakes).

One of the big downsides of Collaborating is that it takes time and energy. If you need to have a Collaborative outcome on a high-stakes issue, start early. Allow plenty of time for it. You want to try to avoid a Compromise outcome.

Avoid avoidance

Compromise when there's not enough time to do a Collaborative deal, or where perhaps it's not worth the effort. Meeting someone halfway is better than no deal, and we live to work together another day.

Accommodate when you want to build the relationship and it's low-stakes. Let them have their way on something you don't need to worry about, so that you can build up your bank of points and cash them in later on high-stakes Collaborative issues.

A word of warning on the Accommodator response: use it sparingly and be a little unpredictable, so that people realize this is a one-off.

Avoiding – is it ever a good choice? Not often, but it does work in some situations:

- When you need more information ('let me come back to you').
- When emotions are running high ('let's take a break and talk again after lunch').
- When you know you can't win and can't afford to let someone else win. If you see no prospect of getting what you want, try to make the issue go away entirely (by being creative) so that no one ends up with it.

Using your self-awareness

I'd like to focus here on Avoiding and Accommodating, as these are the two profiles with most benefit to be gained by a change in behaviour.

Introverts tend to think before they talk, and it takes them more energy to say what's on their mind than extroverts. Keeping your thoughts to yourself would seem to be a logical fit on to Avoiding, wouldn't it?

Whatever the reason for having an Avoidance preference, try to avoid it. Avoid Avoidance! Why? Because conflict is like a seed: it grows. If you avoid a conflict, it sometimes goes away, but most times it doesn't. Then it gets bigger and, before you know it, your seed is now a tree and needs a chainsaw to cut it down. Far better to pull it out when it's a seedling.

If Accommodating is your thing, recognize when being helpful isn't a good idea. Often people come to you to ask for things because they expect you to say yes (because you usually do). When you start to ask more questions and don't say yes straight away, they may realize you're not such a pushover and may stop asking you.

Avoid avoidance

Some other conflict-handling tips

When dealing with conflict, ask questions that begin with who, what, why, where, when and how?

- Who says?
- What room for manoeuvre do you have?
- Why can't we do that?
- Where does it say we're not allowed to?
- When do you need it by?
- How important is it?

As they talk, you're calming down, moving into discovery mode and planning your options (while at the same time listening, of course). Then summarize what they said. This shows that you listened, removes misunderstanding and allows you to take control.

Never respond if you've lost control. Some people will deliberately insult you in order to have you lose control. If you feel this happening the chances are you won't respond as well as if you were in control so it's better to get out of the situation if you can. Put the phone down. Walk out of the room. By all means draft the email response, but save it, don't send it. I guarantee you that when you read it the next morning, you'll change it.

Talk straight. Be as clear and direct as you can. If you have bad news, get to the point and move into exploration mode as quickly as you can.

So what? Over to you...

1. What's your preferred conflict-handling style, and what does that mean for your relationships at work? (You could go online and take the TKI test to help you work this out.)

2. How might you experiment with using a different style to your usual one this week, and how might that change the outcome?

3. What potential conflicts are you avoiding right now, and how might you address them so they don't grow into something harder to tackle?

Day 7
Think! Working Smart model

Introduction

Let's assume you're not looking for ways to work even harder. You're probably already tired and don't relax enough or take sufficient breaks. We need to work smarter, not harder.

'Thinking is for dummies!'

We live in a fast-paced world, and it's getting faster. We want answers, we want results and we want them *now*! Which means working smarter, not harder.

Working Smart

There are three steps to getting things done:

1. Doing it (Action).
2. Working out how to do it (Process).
3. Clarifying what we're supposed to be doing and why (Context).

I call this model Working Smart.

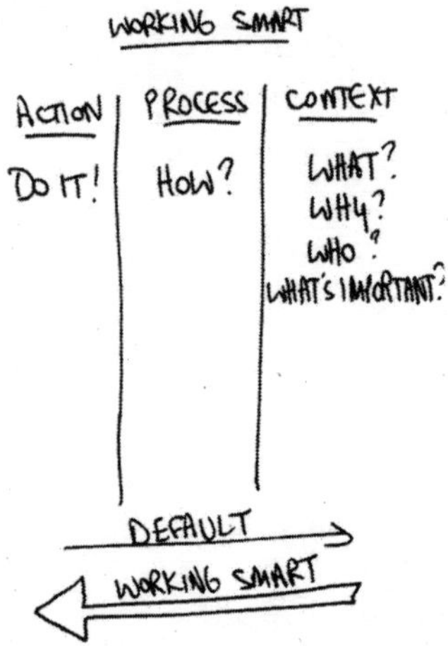

WORKING SMART

ACTION	PROCESS	CONTEXT
DO IT!	HOW?	WHAT? WHY? WHO? WHAT'S IMPORTANT?

DEFAULT →
← WORKING SMART

All too often at work we start with the Action step, working out how to do the project as we go along and not bothering to check what exactly we're supposed to do or why until we finish (if at all). This is the equivalent of jumping out of an airplane and working out how to open the parachute on the way

Think! Working Smart model

down. It's exciting but risky and a bit stressful!

We allow our adaptive unconscious mind to leap to conclusions and we don't give the conscious mind enough time to work things out. Why? Because we're *always* up against time pressure, because time is money. It's peer pressure, too, and people don't have the courage to say, 'Hold on a minute, let's think this through.'

We can indeed get more done by slowing down.

The Working Smart model is great for meetings, and for projects, of course, and it works superbly when negotiating. The key to Working Smart is to read my diagram by starting on the right and working to the left.

Let's explore this in more detail.

What (and how) to clarify at the start: Step 1

The Context stage is where we clarify the important things so that we can get it right first time.

- What are we doing? (Not as silly as it sounds. Do not proceed until you've answered this.)
- Why are we doing this? (Not always a popular question – the answer might be 'we're not sure'.)
- Who is it for? (Know your customer.)

- What's important? (What criteria will the customer use to evaluate it?)
- How will it be used? (Who is the customer's customer and what do they care about?)
- What resources do we have? (Who's done it before, who has ideas?)

How do you respond to the idea of asking these questions? Some people tell me they resist them at first. Asking questions like these brings an open mind to the task. You're providing crucial facilitation to the group, and helping others to save time and Work Smart.

Another reason for not asking these questions is the fear of being seen as 'difficult'. One way to overcome this is to explain why you're asking and for it not to sound like an attack on anyone: 'There's something I'm not clear on here, do you mind if I just ask for the sake of my understanding: why are we doing this?' Position your questions in a collaborative way.

Agreeing your Process: Step 2

Don't proceed to Step 2 (the Process stage) until you're all happy that you have answers to the Context questions.

Think! Working Smart model

You know *what* you're going to do, now work out *how*. Again, you don't have to be the project leader to pose this question. It can sound quite inoffensive and you can ask it as a member of the group: 'How do we think we should go about this?'

Brainstorm some options. Try not to run with the first idea in the interest of saving time. If someone wants to push on to the Action (doing it) stage, hold them back: 'Before we do that, let's just check to see if anyone else has an alternative suggestion.'

Once you have a Process in mind, check back to Step 1 to make sure that it ties in to all the information you have about the requirement. Then move on to Step 3.

At last! Action: Step 3

This is most people's favourite stage. Why? Because it's the sweet spot. It's where our expertise kicks in and where we feel as though at last we're making progress. This bit is measurable and we begin to see some outputs.

A final point to make about Working Smart: once you get into the Action stage, don't stay locked into it. Go back to Step 2 now and then to check your Process is still fit for purpose. If it isn't, check against Step 1 and see whether you need to adapt the Process, and if so, modify the Process accordingly. Now that's what I call agile working.

So what? Over to you...

1. Think back to a recent time you worked with a group on an activity or project. How quickly did you 'jump out of the airplane' (i.e. get in Action) before working out the Context or Process? Why do you think that is?

Think! Working Smart model

2. What phrases could you use in future to help your team avoid jumping to Action too quickly, without sounding 'difficult'?

3. Think of a project that's currently in the Action phase. How might you loop back to Steps 1 and 2 to check that the Process is still appropriate?

Day 8

Listen more

Introduction

Genuine listening will build trust and will help both you and the other person.

Trouble is, it's not easy. It requires self-discipline and time (although in the long term it saves time) and it requires us to pay genuine attention to other people. Nancy Kline suggests that we're conditioned to not listen and that we have to consciously create a Thinking Environment – one where people have a chance to fully express themselves and work out their own solutions. This is a very different one from the default leadership style in most organizations, which is essentially the result of what she calls Male Conditioning.

Nancy sums up the difference using this table:[4]

Thinking Environment	Male Conditioning
Listen	Take over and talk
Ask incisive questions	Know everything
Establish equality	Assume superiority
Appreciate	Criticize
Be at ease	Control
Encourage	Compete
Feel	Toughen
Supply accurate information	Lie
Humanize the place	Conquer the place
Create diversity	Deride difference

Listening shows respect: you're acknowledging the other person, which is often all they want.

The introverts welcome it

Introverts (who get energy from inside rather than outside stimuli) are wired differently to extroverts (who welcome stimulation from outside). In her book *Quiet: The power of the introvert in a world that can't stop talking*, Susan Cain says that:

Listen more

'Introverts have the same physical nervous system as Extroverts, but they have a different sensitivity to stimuli. Their nervous system reacts more to all forms of stimulation. They work best where there is less stimulation. Extroverts do the opposite. They get listless and bored where there is not enough stimulation.'[5]

Extroverts think out loud and are happy to do the talking in meetings. Introverts tend to think about what they say before they say it and often need space to get their thoughts out – maybe via a second sentence. When an extrovert interrupts them or jumps in too quickly, the introvert doesn't get their point across, which leads to misunderstandings and frustration and often disengagement by the introvert.

If you're an extrovert, consider which of your key stakeholders is an introvert and think about how to allow more space so you can access their contribution. If you're an introvert, how can you ensure your voice gets heard? Does someone need some feedback? Do you need to be more visible in meetings? Do you need to stop people from interrupting or ignoring you?

It helps others to grow

What are you looking for from your manager? What's the number one attribute you'd like to see in them?

Google researched this question extensively in 2013 in what they called Project Oxygen.[6] From thousands of internal interviews, they found that most people were looking for a manager who is a good coach.

Running a close second came 'Empowers me. Does not micromanage.' This implies a complete rethink of how managers should prioritize their time. If you're a manager, how much of a priority are you making coaching?

This is based on a slide I use when I'm training people on coaching:

- When I ask you to listen and you start giving advice, you've not done what I've asked.
- When I ask you to listen and you start telling me why I shouldn't feel the way I do, you're invalidating my feelings.
- When I ask you to listen and you interrupt and start trying to solve my problem, I feel underestimated and disempowered.
- When I ask you to listen and you start telling me what I need to do, I feel offended, pressured and controlled.

Listen more

- When I ask you to listen, it doesn't mean I'm helpless. I may be faltering, depressed or discouraged, but I'm not helpless.
- When I ask you to listen and you do things that I can and need to do for myself, you hurt my self-esteem.
- But when you accept the way I feel, then I don't need to spend time and energy trying to defend myself or convince you, and I can focus on figuring out why I feel the way I feel and what to do about it.
- And when I do that, I don't need advice, just support, trust and encouragement.
- Please remember that what you think are irrational feelings always make sense if you take time to listen and understand me.

We can all be coaches, and if we do it well we help others to grow while at the same time learning ourselves. Good coaching is rare, and I know of no organization where managers see coaching as a priority.

Too many people think when someone asks for coaching, their role is to problem-solve and 'fix' the coaching requirement as quickly as possible. Their preferred coaching style is directive – making suggestions and locking in on the answer to the 'problem'.

Providing answers for people disempowers them (infantilizes them) and causes stunted growth.

A great way to help people to step up and take on more responsibility is to coach them using a listening style. Caroline Webb describes this brilliantly:

> 'When someone is telling you about a problem and we leap in to offer advice, a paradox arises: it's all too easy to leave the other person feeling bombarded rather than soothed. "Have you done this? What about that?" Inadvertently, we can even make the other person feel judged, as if they should have spotted the answer themselves. If that happens, their brain is likely to register our well-intentioned help as a kind of threat – which makes them less creative in their own thinking about the problem. By the end of the discussion, they are left mumbling, "Well, I guess I'll go and do all those things then."'[7]

Avoiding this will involve asking some wonderfully simple 'coaching' questions, such as:

- Why is this important?
- What do you think?
- What have you tried so far?
- What are the options?

Listen more

- What are you going to do differently?

Some of the best coaches I know are introverts. They can be great coaches because they're more natural listeners.

Listening provides you with options

The core skill in both negotiation and conflict handling is the ability to listen and to ask good questions. Research suggests that the most effective negotiators are those who talk least and ask the best questions.

An important technique is to get the other person talking. Here are a few tips on how to do that:

- Defer to their expertise.
- Set a range without making an offer.
- Expose their underlying interests.
- Ask them 'why?' several times in succession.
- Ask them to summarize.

How do you listen?

Funny if you think about it. We get taught how to talk, read and write when we're young, but no one teaches us the other (and arguably most important) communication skill, which is how to listen. Pity really. The world might be a better place if we were better at it.

I'm talking about listening to understand. Not listening to identify when there's a gap in the transmission so we can reply. Not listening in order to respond. Not listening in order to disagree. Our aim is to understand the other person's position in order to empathize and recognize our starting point for the conversation.

Caroline Webb has some good suggestions to make:[8]

- Let the other person set the topic (because it's about them, not you).
- Don't interrupt (this is *so* hard!).
- Maintain eye contact. When you avert your eyes, even for a moment, it can break rapport.
- Keep them talking. Nod. Smile. Ask, 'What else?'

Remember that introverts sometimes need a few attempts at getting their thinking out. Pause to allow them time to go on to say more. This is often when they'll say what's really on their mind.

If appropriate, make notes. Summarize: play it back to them and make it clear that this is to

Listen more

check your understanding. 'Let me just check I've understood properly: you're saying...'

Create rapport. When you have rapport, both people will find it easier to communicate and to think. Match their posture, gestures, energy level, facial expressions. Match the volume of their voice and even the speed. Become like the other person by modifying yourself. Subconsciously the other person will find you easier to deal with because you're more like themselves. That will help both of you.

✏️ So what? Over to you...

1. Be honest: what are you like as a listener? When do you find it hardest?

2. How can you look out for poor listening in meetings and do something about it; for example, when someone is interrupted or not invited to speak?

Listen more

3. What might happen if you allow some silence now and then? How can you try that out this week?

Day 9
Meet intelligently

Introduction

Let's look now at how to be more intelligent about using that scarce and sacred resource – time. Ineffective and inappropriate meetings are, people tell me, their number one time stealer each and every week.

Note that I'm talking here about meetings that are designed to move things forward – get some decisions and some agreed actions. There are other types of meetings that are more of a 'group hug': share some best practice, check in with each other, acknowledge some achievements, learn something new and walk away feeling motivated and inspired to carry on. These are a perfectly valid use of time but they're not what I'm focusing on here.

What a waste of time!

Over the years various studies, including my own, have shown that there are high levels of dissatisfaction with meetings. Biggest causes of angst are:

- Unclear objectives and poor or non-existent agendas, and therefore wandering off-topic.
- Lack of self-discipline and mutual respect.
- Poor or non-existent timekeeping.
- Poor or non-existent preparation.
- Inappropriate use of time (e.g. presenting information that could and should have been circulated and read beforehand).
- Unclear results, including decisions made and who does what.
- Lack of respect for others' time (including acknowledging time zones).
- Irrelevance to attendees.

All of these are easily fixed and you'll find that if you start to model a new way of running meetings, others quickly begin to follow.

No agenda = no meeting!

Meetings without agendas are at best going to be inefficient and at worst a waste of time. If you provide a focus for the discussion you'll be better able to keep people on-topic and manage the time.

My first suggestion is that you do not attend meetings without agendas.

I repeat. Do *not* attend meetings without agendas.

Obviously the ones you organize are included in this. But for other people's meetings, ask what the agenda is. If there is none, you could ask for one, and if one isn't forthcoming, you can politely decline on the grounds that you don't know whether it's relevant to you. You can ask them to send you the minutes of the meeting so that you can decide whether to attend next time.

Give people time to provide input into the agenda before the meeting. That way they buy in and can give the items some thought before they come (very welcome by the introverts).

Because the agenda is pre-agreed, you're now able to shut down agenda hijackers (you know, the person who ten minutes before the end of the meeting drops

Meet intelligently

a bomb of some sort, which you don't have time to discuss properly and throws everything into confusion).

If people don't have the discipline to ask for their item to be on the agenda, it doesn't get discussed. In other words, don't allow AOB (Any Other Business). We only allow Adults in these meetings.

Manage the time

Have you ever noticed how when you put a timescale on something people seem to work to it? This works very well with agendas. Put how long you're allowing for the topic on the agenda. And then appoint someone to be the timekeeper and ask them to interrupt when you're five minutes from the deadline. I promise you, it will focus people's minds.

Set the objective

As well as adding timing to the agenda, state an objective for the agenda item.

Capture the decisions and agreed actions

Meetings are designed to produce action. Capture what's agreed so that you can review progress next time. If people know that they're going to be held accountable it tends to make a difference to whether they do what they said they would.

Nominate someone to take the minutes. They can do this during the meeting using a simple spreadsheet with four columns: Item, Action, By whom, By when. This can then be circulated straight after the meeting and reviewed as the first item on the agenda at the next meeting. If you choose to not do what you said you would, be ready to explain yourself next time.

Encourage participation

When we invite people to a meeting the intention is generally to invite their contribution.

You may have an imbalance in the contribution levels, often because the vocal ones get in first, excluding the more thoughtful or softly spoken ones (or those for whom the language for the meeting isn't their first language and they're having to process everything twice).

There are several ways you can get around this. Nancy Kline suggests you kick off the meeting by asking *everyone* to say what's going well in their work or in the group's work. This gives everyone a turn, and creates a positive atmosphere.[9] If people know they're required to contribute, they'll be prepared to think and remain engaged.

Nancy is a passionate advocate of not allowing interruptions. Not interrupting will save time in the meeting. It also makes sense because often people need time to articulate their idea and can't get it over in just one sentence. And usually the meaning of their point is at the end of the sentence anyway, so if you interrupt you don't fully understand their point. Let them finish before anyone responds. This device works equally well in virtual meetings, of course, and the fact that everyone knows they'll be asked to contribute may make it more likely that they remain engaged rather than answering emails.

Are you facilitating or leading?

I hear a lot of confusion about facilitation and what it involves. People think they're facilitating when in fact they're leading. This can be damaging.

Facilitating involves helping a group to work out a solution to something. Leading involves, as the name suggests, leading the group towards a solution. Sometimes we need to put on both hats during a meeting. Of the two, facilitation is much more of an art form. It requires judgement and agile thinking.

I like to think of facilitating as being like a referee in a game of soccer. Good referees are invisible when they can be and blow the whistle only when they need to. Crucially, they do not kick the ball! It's the job of the two teams to play the game and abide by the rules (i.e. stick to the agenda or the agreed objective of the discussion). When they stop doing so, the referee needs to blow the whistle.

In other words, if you're facilitating, you don't have an opinion. You're there to facilitate the group in carrying out the task: to make it easy for them (the word has its roots in Latin, *facilis* – easy).

Once you stop having an opinion you'll find it easier to observe the process the group is using and to help them when you need to. You create an Adult-to-Adult relationship with the group, as opposed to a Parent–Child one, which is often what you get when you lead a discussion.

Tips

- If you're a facilitator, delegate someone else as scribe, thus freeing yourself up to observe the 'game' and check that the process is working.
- Write down – verbatim – what people say – not what you think they meant. If you distort

their words into yours you're judging them and positioning yourself as a mind reader or an expert. When you've finished writing it all down, you can review the list – if there's something ridiculous up there, normally someone in the group will spot it and call it out.

How to get things off to a flying start

Let's look now at my tried-and-tested model for getting off to a flying start for meetings and for kicking off a presentation. The idea is to clarify the five things that people need to know before they can get into the discussion (or listen to the presentation). Think of the following: Interest, Need, Timing, Route Map, Objective (which helpfully make the acronym INTRO).

I	INTEREST	Say something that will enable people to tune in, such as, 'Let me read you this complaint I received yesterday.'

N	NEED	Point out to them why we're having this discussion. Some form of emotional appeal is always helpful here, such as fear, excitement or pride.
T	TIMING	People worry about how long this is going to take. So tell them.
R	ROUTE MAP	They also worry about what's going to happen. Tell them the agenda and how you're going to cover it.
O	OBJECTIVE	State the objective and keep it SMART (i.e. as concrete and measurable as possible).

You might want to prepare the INTRO in advance so you have something to say on each point. Practise it if necessary, then when you stand up you just hit your mental 'play' button and out will pop the perfect opening few words.

So what? Over to you…

1. How can you ensure that there's an agenda for every meeting you run and that you're invited to? Think too about how to manage the resistance you'll inevitably face on this!

2. How might you use the INTRO model to kick off a discussion or a presentation?

3. If you attend a regular meeting that's badly run, how might you suggest a review of the meeting at the end, and what suggestions for improvement might you make?

Day 10

Know yourself

Open your mind to the idea that you may not know yourself as well as you should, and this might be a missed opportunity for both you and your employer. Once you've found a way to know yourself better, do something with the information.

Play to your strengths

Knowing your strengths (and recognizing your weaknesses), building them and maximizing their impact is a much more productive and fruitful way to develop yourself than putting energy into overcoming your weaknesses.

Know yourself

Creating room for your strengths

How well do you know your strengths, and how well are you able to deploy them in your role as it currently stands?

If you've answered those two questions and have recognized that your strengths aren't fully harnessed in your current role, what should you do about it?

It could be that your only option is to find a new role. But let's assume for now that you're not ready to quit, but you'd like things to change.

One idea is to make a proposal for modifying your role so that you can play to your strengths more. If you do this in a way that results in a collaborative response, both you and your boss stand to benefit. Assuming there's room for negotiation on those job components, what do you now have capacity to do that you didn't before, and how could that replacement activity play to your strengths?

Playing to your strengths doesn't, of course, necessarily require a renegotiation of your role. You might find yourself using a new approach to the job and getting better results because you have more energy.

Doing things that we're naturally drawn to and that motivate us does wonders for career mojo. There's a big difference between having a duty or obligation to do something and wanting to do something because you're naturally drawn to it.

Know your team

Anthony Landale (a brilliant facilitator I knew from some breakthrough coaching he gave me) ran an exercise for my team, which I invite you to do for yourself. It's hugely powerful. He invited us to think of a particular moment when we were at our personal best: what he calls our 'Best Self'. What particular strengths were we using? How did it feel to be doing it this way? What was the impact on others?

As each of us shared our story we felt the team 'glue' between us strengthen and we developed a real appreciation of each other's strengths. Someone talked about the run-up to their wedding, another about the day his father died.

When a whole team knows their strengths, you can allocate work more intelligently. You can make up project teams with a good balance of strengths. You can use the information to recruit more intelligently as well.

Know yourself

A word about introversion

Introverts get energy from inside themselves, through being quiet. They think deeply and in silence, stick with problems much longer than extroverts do and tend to be less vocal in meetings.

The Western world tends to have a bias towards extroversion. High levels of interaction with other people are encouraged – when you were young your parents probably told you to go out and play with the other kids rather than stay in your bedroom on your games console. The workplace tends to encourage people to meet, interact and bounce ideas around.

But introverts hate all that jazzed-up stuff! A noisy brainstorm is the least effective way to get ideas out of an introvert. Far better to give them the problem to solve in advance of the meeting and let them come along having given it some thought.

If you're an introvert, your working environment might be affecting your mojo. Interacting with others drains you. You can do it and come across as perfectly sociable; it's just that you prefer more peace and quiet and time to think. Might you be more productive working from home if that's possible? Or are there options for working in a quieter part of the office when you need to do some deep thinking?

The chameleon approach

Knowing yourself and understanding that others will have different preferences to yours is only a part of the story. Applying this information is where emotional intelligence kicks in. You can't change the other person, but you can influence their response to you by adapting your own behaviour.

The animal of choice for getting more of your own way, it seems to me, is the chameleon, able to adapt to the context where necessary, to become the 'colour' that matches the other person. This involves changes of mindset as well as adapting our style, body language and voice. The truth is, one size does not fit all.

Know yourself

✏️ So what? Over to you...

1. How well is your role suited to your personality type and your personal preferences? If there are elements that you'd be better suited to do more or less of, how might you influence that?

2. If the role is a really bad fit, you may need to face up to looking for a new role. How might you do that?

Know yourself

3. What would it look like to use the 'chameleon' approach when dealing with others with a different style and personality to yours? When and where might you try that out this week?

Conclusion

You'll have gathered from what you've read so far that there's plenty that you can do to make going to work a happier part of your life. I'm sure there's also plenty of stuff that you can do nothing about, and sometimes (maybe often, sadly) it basically just sucks and you have to either put up with it or quit. But in the less extreme situations your mojo can be given a real boost using some of the techniques I've been describing.

If you're realizing that at least some of your unhappiness at work might be self-inflicted, here are a few final thoughts to help you do something about that.

Some popular mojo blockers

These are some of the most popular mojo blockers I've come across. Put a tick against the ones you're particularly prone to.

- Working too hard
- Not sharing

Conclusion

- Doing things that aren't important
- Never taking time to reflect and learn
- Doing everything perfectly
- Being obsessed by deadlines
- Not negotiating
- Not knowing what's required
- Doing things that are no longer relevant or required
- Never saying 'no'
- Not securing the resources needed
- Not being clear on who does what
- Making assumptions
- Keeping the customer at arm's length
- Jumping in too fast
- Not asking enough questions
- Being too available
- Being obsessed with social media
- Add your own……………………………

Which ones do you need to work on?

Adjust your mindset

Your attitude towards any situation is a choice. You choose whether to be angry or to collaborate. You choose to make something a point of principle or to let it go.

I have found that being yourself, with all your vulnerabilities and anxieties, is the best person to be. Trying to fake it and make out you're someone else is not only hard to sustain, it's also rarely a total success – people see through it and then you come across as insincere or inconsistent and they won't trust you. And, worst of all, it's tiring. Yes, there's a time and a place to be someone else, for the purposes of the moment – that meeting with the CEO, that make-or-break client presentation you have to deliver. But not all the time.

Mojo maintenance tips

- Read! Business books, biographies, fiction – anything thought-provoking to broaden your mind. It's hardly surprising if people feel they're slipping out of touch if the only things they read are knee-jerk reactions to news on social media.
  - But here's a worrying thought: are we all losing the ability to read? I find myself totally recognizing what author Michael Harris says in this article titled 'I have forgotten how to read'.[10] 'Turning, one evening, from my phone to a book, I set

myself the task of reading a single chapter in one sitting. Simple. But I couldn't... if I'm being honest – the failure was not a surprise. Paragraphs swirled; sentences snapped like twigs; and sentiments bled out. The usual, these days. I drag my vision across the page and process little. Half an hour later, I throw down the book and watch some Netflix.'

- I'd also just ask you whether you're getting enough sleep? Matthew Walker, who has been studying how sleep affects the human mind and body for two decades, concludes that we're in the midst of a 'catastrophic sleep loss epidemic'.[11] He has discovered powerful links between sleep loss and Alzheimer's, cancer, diabetes, obesity and anxiety. Apparently nearly 50% of us are trying to get by on fewer than six hours of sleep per night.
- Walker has a non-negotiable eight hours every night. There are sound medical reasons for this:
    - 'After just one night of only four or five hours' sleep, your natural killer cells – the ones that attack the cancer cells that appear in your body every day – drop by 70%.'

- In the workplace, lack of sleep has been shown to amplify the reaction of the amygdala – a key part of the brain responsible for triggering anger and rage – by 60%. If you find yourself having emotional outbursts at work, lack of sleep could be the culprit. Is a change of sleep routine something you need to consider?
- Get yourself a mentor or a coach. Someone who has either trodden the same path as you (mentor) or a coach to help you tread your own path. Just having the support and interest of someone independent and objective can be a great boost and a source of wellbeing. (And don't forget that you can coach yourself too whenever you need it – as you've learned through this book!)

It's all too easy to slip into comfortable habits and lose sight of the need to constantly work out our mojo. It really is up to you whether you choose to be proactive or whether you prefer seeing what shows up.

Conclusion

Practical takeaways: Reward, Remind, Repeat

Caroline Webb has some excellent advice on how to make these new approaches stick. She suggests the Reward, Remind, Repeat mantra.[12]

- **Reward:** If you reward yourself with a mental pat on the back and a moment to reflect on what went well, you're more likely to repeat the behaviour.
- **Remind:** Find yourself whatever visual or tactile prompt works best for you, so that the behaviour you're trying to change is prompted in some way by it. This could be a visual reminder on the whiteboard in your office. Or screensavers. Or a photo of the model or excerpt from a book on your phone. Or an object: a talisman of some sort in your pocket. A photo. A piece of art.

I have to work hard at not talking too fast when I present, and one way I do that is by printing out the slides nine per page as a prompt for myself and writing SLOW DOWN or PAUSE at least once per page. It works for me.

Ask a colleague for feedback on the behaviour you're working on, to see whether you're

applying it and what the impact is. It makes you accountable.
- **Repeat:** When you try out these new behaviours, attitudes and beliefs, they may feel clumsy and unnatural because you're breaking old habits that have formed over years.

  Embrace the discomfort! That awkward sensation is a sign that you're trying out something new, and for that you should give yourself an internal round of applause.

And finally...

Speaking of internal rounds of applause, give yourself one for reading this book. You've acknowledged you want to work on yourself and do something about your workplace happiness, and you've taken the first step.

Now let's make sure it's not been a waste of time! Please, please, please take some action to get started, and don't do it tomorrow. Today would be better. As the saying goes, 'If not now, then when?'

One action you could take very easily indeed is to share this book with someone else. Go on, spread the love! And spread the word: who else could do with a mojo boost?

I wish you every success in the world.

Endnotes

[1] S. Sinek, *Start with Why: How great leaders inspire everyone to take action* (Penguin, 2011).

[2] Department of Economics, University of Sheffield, 'Workplace trust key factor in productivity', at Sheffield ac.uk (21 August 2015) www.sheffield.ac.uk/faculty/social-sciences/news/workplace-trust-1.499084 (accessed February 2018).

[3] K. W. Thomas and R. H. Kilmann, Thomas-Kilmann Conflict Mode Instrument (TKI) [Database record]. APA PsycTests (1974). https://doi.org/10.1037/t02326-000

[4] N. Kline, *Time to Think* (Cassell, 2002), p. 91.

[5] S. Cain, *Quiet: the power of the introvert in a world that can't stop talking* (Penguin, 2013).

[6] D. A. Garvin, 'How Google sold its managers on management' at HBR.com (December 2013) https://hbr.org/2013/12/how-google-sold-its-engineers-on-management (accessed February 2018).

[7] C. Webb, *How To Have a Good Day* (Macmillan, 2016).

[8] C. Webb, *How To Have a Good Day* (Macmillan, 2016).

[9] N. Kline, *Time to Think* (Cassell, 2002).

[10] M. Harris, 'I have forgotten how to read' at Theglobe andmail.com (February 2018) www.theglobeandmail.com/opinion/i-have-forgotten-how-toread/article37921379/ (accessed March 2018).

[11] M. Walker, 'The sleep deprivation epidemic' at thersa.org (23 October 2017) www.thersa.org/discover/videos/event-videos/2017/10/matthew-walker-on-the-sleepdeprivation-epidemic?gclid=EAIaIQobChMI486_r7ql2QIVr7ft Ch3sWAsKEAAYA SAAEgJq2PD_BwE (accessed August 2024).

[12] C. Webb, *How To Have a Good Day* (Macmillan, 2016).

Enjoyed this?
Then you'll love…

My Job Isn't Working! 10 proven ways to boost your career mojo by Michael Brown

If you're a typical mid-career worker in a typical enterprise – been around a while, employs more than a handful of people – the chances are you're being squeezed. Hard. You're under pressure like never before, coming at you from all directions. It's getting worse, and the prospects are worse still. You've been asked to do more with less for years, and there's nothing left to give. You can't trust people, you feel insecure, and the job seems a bit pointless. You've given up trying to fix the crappy processes you have to work with, because it's easier to disengage.

Meanwhile the outside world appears to have gone mad, you're worrying about when a robot is going to take your job, work-life balance is an outdated concept, and you no longer know how to switch off. You may well want out, but can't work out how to do it, so you're stuck.

Your career mojo – the engine that keeps you motoring at work – needs servicing or, worse still, it's broken down.

The great news is that there's a way through this. The engine can be repaired. You *can* find meaning and fulfilment in the work you do.

In this book, Michael Brown reveals the ten techniques he has used to help thousands of mid-career workers boost their career mojo. Discover the simple changes you can make to transform your work life. Using real-life stories and examples, he explains in concise and pragmatic terms how to make every day a good day at the office.

Michael Brown runs his own training consultancy, specializing in building leadership, team development and negotiation skills. He has been working with complex international organizations for over 20 years, helping people thrive in a rapidly evolving and increasingly dysfunctional workplace.

Other 6-Minute Smarts titles

Write to Think (based on *Exploratory Writing* by Alison Jones)

No-Nonsense PR (based on *Hype Yourself* by Lucy Werner)

Do Change Better (based on *How to be a Change Superhero* by Lucinda Carney)

Mastering People Management (based on *Mission: To Manage* by Marianne Page)

Present Like a Pro (based on *Executive Presentations* by Jacqui Harper)

Look out for more titles coming soon! Visit www.practicalinspiration.com for all our latest titles.